CLICK AND CONNECT

KAREN HONNOR

DEDICATION

This is dedicated to family and friends, to all who have struggled and those who have been there to lend a helping hand.

CONTENTS

ACKNOWLEDGMENTS

To my family – Stuart, Matthew and Zoe for their continued support through good and bad times and for the numerous times you have reassured and encouraged me. For all the moments where we have tried to hold it together, in this year like no other. We are all still taking one day at a time and for now that is enough.

To my Mum – Mary, who's been shielding for a year. She's an inspiration. Waiting for the day we can eat chips by the sea.

To friends who have a made a difference this year – online, on the phone, dropping items on the doorstep or through other socially distanced moments. Little gestures go so much further than ever before and I will be forever grateful for so many moments that friendship has brought my way.

To connections – in many forms. When it is so easy to withdraw further and further into our shell, the connections we continue to make are crucial. They inspire me and lift me at my darkest moments.

To Clare Lawrence-Simms and the Community Harmony Scarf project for inspiring the story – Ruby's Ribbons. A truly inspirational lady who strives to spread her positivity and help others wherever she goes.

To Zoe for the illustrations featured within these pages.

RAINBOWS

Among life's debris you may come across the occasional glint of gold. When you find it, no matter how small, hold it up to let it shimmer.

PLAYING WITH WORDS

I have been playing with words for years now – scripts and poems mainly, more recently blog posts and stories. The more I write, the more I think like a writer and find a reassurance and comfort by retreating into my pages. Writing down my thoughts has always been therapeutic. At this moment in time, it has been so much more. It has helped me to make connections with people. Such connections have formed friendships, given support and started conversations.

I have channeled this year's experiences into my writing. There has been a lot of nostalgia attached to them as reflection has found me focusing on memories and those thoughts that I am sure most of us share right now, to be able to get to a point soon where we can begin to build memories together again.

This is my collection of words from this year. Playing with different thoughts and ideas, mostly through poems but also in other ways to express emotions, concerns, hopes and wishes. The thread attached to all of these is CONNECTION. Whether within the construct of our social bubbles, the bonds we have shared with colleagues in our current work situations or the friendships and support received virtually, through one screen or another.

The nature of our connections may be changing but they remain central to our well-being, central to what makes us human. We all need that connection. I hope that the writing within these pages makes a connection with its readers in a way that proves uplifting, supportive and ultimately positive.

We all need to find our sunny moments among the dark clouds.

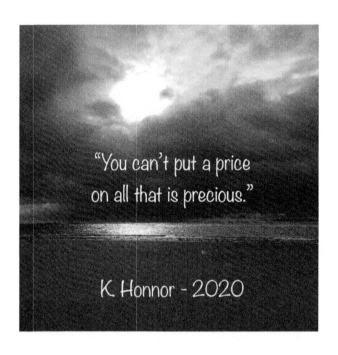

Quote from 'Unravelling – A Tale of Strength, Love and Dementia.'
December 2020

RECOGNISING RAINBOWS

This is a blog post that I wrote last year, during our first lockdown period. It feels a good place to start this collection, looking back to the time when it was written, when there seemed to be a more united atmosphere and the rainbows popping up all around us, symbolised hope. I like to think that they still do and that we can keep striving for that necessary UNITY in our COMMUNITY. I saw that phrase somewhere on Twitter recently and it's a definite goal to aim for...

***

In these dark and worrying times the growing proliferation of rainbows displayed on windows, chalked on pavements and garden paths, or woven into fences bring a message of hope. Most have been created by those children who are now trying to make sense of the growing insular world that they find themselves in. Other examples, are the work of adults who similarly are at a loss to comprehend what is happening and how any of us are supposed to behave at the moment.

I suppose these rainbows are tangible – an identifiable positive image and therein lies their hope. For those readers unfamiliar with this movement, pictures of rainbows have started appearing in neighbourhoods in the UK so that the children taking their permitted exercise can look out for them, count them, and also see that others are doing the same as they are. Examples I have seen have started to be customised to include greetings or messages of gratitude to the postman, carers and the NHS. They are a slowly spreading expression of community.

In a recent book I wrote a chapter called 'I can sing a rainbow' where I examined my coloured memories. Have you ever played that game where you have to say what immediately comes to mind as you are given a colour name? I started playing that really as I wrote my chapter and found each colour sparked off my memories so that I found I could recall a whole myriad of experiences, of places, people and events. Perhaps this is why the rainbow phenomena resonated with me? It brought me back to writing that chapter and thinking of all those coloured memories – "Times of happiness and of people that mattered to me, who were significant in my life."

There is a quote often seen on Pinterest boards and gifts bought to uplift the recipient. I will paraphrase it here as

"No rain, no rainbows."

At the moment, we are all under a whole lot of cloud so it is little wonder that we are searching for rainbows. Each rainbow we find along the way of a permitted daily exercise signals the promise to the end of our collective confinement. It recognises the kindnesses being shown by neighbours, friends, families and complete strangers. When you sift through the scary news on social media, there are examples you can find of such kindnesses. A meal or treat being dropped off at the door of a vulnerable or elderly person. A young lad giving the last bag of pasta that he had taken off the shelf to a stranger in the shop who looked like they needed it more. That friend or relative that hasn't been in touch for ages, picking up the phone or sending a text message just to see if you are okay.

This strange limbo time has got me thinking about a lot of things – sometimes in the middle of the night, a practice I am trying to stop as I don't want to add insomnia to the list of items to be concerned about. However, I wanted to focus on the positive in all of this. When you can't get out to find these rainbows scattered through your neighbourhood, you can turn your attention to what is immediately around you. There are four adults in our house, three of whom have one level or another of identified vulnerability. One is trying to work from home and concentrate upon all that entails, whilst the household, including an attention-seeking dog, goes on around him. It is safe to say that tensions are forming, moods are rising and falling and being able to concentrate on anything is proving difficult as time goes on.

Yet, I am recognising the rainbows amongst these clouds. We are engaging in conversation when, given our previous freedoms, some of us would have been off doing our own things. We are planning, cooking and sharing family meals together – much less of the everyone doing their own thing, eating at different times, passing like ships around the metaphorical harbour of the dining table. None of us are entirely sure of the right measures to take but we are trying to look out for each other, balancing feeling informed by the news and social media posts with getting overwhelmed by them all. We are trying new things – planting vegetable seeds in makeshift pots on the window sill, cooking some items from scratch that we haven't done before, developing our tech skills because there isn't someone else to rely on to pop in and do it for us. I am sure there will be much more. I am even being initiated into the world of Marvel and finally getting around to watching the films. That has resulted in another rainbow – family film time is becoming another regular feature. For those who know me, I have a lot of classic film titles to catch up on which is strange for someone married to film industry man!

Yes, there is a lot that is scary – sometimes so much so that to haul yourself out of bed in the morning is a real achievement. I am not trying to paint a rose-tinted picture of life on this limbo lockdown and I am sure it is going to prove more testing the longer that it goes on. But if we keep looking down and focusing on all that is grey and gloomy, the clouds that can easily fill our time, then we miss out on the moments that matter. We don't recognise the rainbows. I have recently managed to publish a poetry chapbook and I have used the rainbow analogy for one particular poem which I include below.

Remember all those moments that you are missing? I wonder what colours they are - get your paintbrush ready, for there will be lots more to come on the other side of this. Be ready to paint a masterpiece.

Red became my confidence, my shield to face the world,
Stepping out in red shoes and lipstick to reassure,
Unleashing an inner bounce to squash the voice of doubt,
Grabbing that attitude along with my outfit to go out.

Orange is my autumn, my smouldering glow,
Taking comfort in what I have and I know I can do,
The warmth from a sunset, the embers from the coal,
The satsuma sweetness from a fresh fruit bowl.

Yellow is bright, it is light touching my soul just when I need it,
The tenacious dandelion clinging on defiantly,
It is loud, a moment of allowing myself to be proud,
Not being afraid to stand out from the crowd.

Green is refreshing, signalling the hope of warmer times,
The new shoots of spring, a lawn carpet cushioning my toes,
The get set go, fresh salads and cool lime,
Raising a long stemmed glass in a moment of time.

Blue is my calm, my reflection when I just need some space,
Breathing slowly to look at the sky and relax,
Floating away in a mermaid lagoon,
Wishing I could return to that cool pool soon.

Indigo and violet are my conjuring of a nostalgic haze,
'Purple Rain' reminiscing, a Cadbury chocolate wrap,
The swirling tie-dye, an amethyst ring,
Lavender and heather on scented air sing.

I'm recognising rainbows amongst my every day,
Finding comfort in the shine that a fleeting moment brings,
For the darkest storms will break and then come to an end,
And amongst the shadows waiting are the tools to heal and mend.

IN THE MOMENT

Recognise what gives you comfort,

List the things that bring you joy,

Hold those close who make a difference,

Seek contentment as your ploy,

Look to nature for its beauty,

Look within to find the key,

Be forgiving and get living,

Find your peace and simply be.

COFFEE TIME

Shall we go for a coffee?
A little hope in a cup,
Share a story, a giggle
To keep spirits up.

Frothy milk over spilling,
Along with a smile,
Placing worries and problems
Aside for a while.

Sit snug in a corner,
Latte nestled in hands,
And let our minds wander
To long golden sands.

Shall we go for a coffee?
Maybe add a sweet treat,
While laughter and friendship
Have their time to meet.

LITTLE GEMS

The sun's shining,
Sky is blue,
Bird hopped by my window as I washed the dishes.

Eggs in stock,
And toilet roll,
Flour dropped on the doorstep by a friend.

Baked a cake,
Favourite mug for coffee,
Flopped upon the sofa to watch something new on the TV.

Mum's safe and well,
Neighbours wave,
Work stopped to share a joke with the children over dinner.

Dog snuggles,
Radio playing,
Ideas popped as pen flows across pages of a new notebook.

Mini moments,
Little gifts and gems,
Spirit topped up and ready to begin another day.

GARDEN SPOT

My dog sits in her favourite spot
Eating winds that tickle her face,
The family know it as her place,
Whenever any sun shines,
She sits and surveys her garden.

Bees may pass by,
The lavender stems sway,
A few flowers flourish in ramshackle pots,
And unless a brazen fox strays by,
She sits with her view of her garden,
Content to stay in her favourite spot.

GOOD TIMES

Strawberries and prosecco
Giggles with good friends
Marshmallows on the barbecue
Evenings with no ends

Laughter with the family
Popcorn and a drink
Lazy days in summer haze
Where no-one needs to think

Walks along the shoreline
Picnics in the sun
Treasure all such moments
Each and every one

The painting below was created by my daughter, Zoe, and given to me on Mothers' Day 2020 – the first Sunday of our new lockdown existence. For that reason, along with the subject matter, it holds a special place in my heart. A promise of good times ahead, a summer break in Cornwall where we can maybe spot a camper van or two while we listen to the sea.

Acrylic on canvas – by Zoe Honnor.

SEASONS

Seasons turn so quickly – catch hold of a moment or two as they pass by.

CROCUS KISS

A little bit of spring has sprung upon my windowsill,
A little hope and colour,
A smile.

A promise of more to come,
A little crocus kiss – the flush of spring.

Resplendent,
Rich purple petals, soft against the tiles of white,
Delicate but definite,
A crocus kiss delight.

BUBBLES

Bubbles - used to be beautiful,
A word that conjured childhood
Freedom,
Flight,
Floating upon a cloudless day

Wondrous delight on little faces
Chasing
Following and then...

Hand held still, in suspense
To hold a single bubble
Upon a fingertip

For each bursting bubble,
A race to dip a wand anew,
Wave a stream,
Cascade them,
Watch their pathway to the sky,
Iridescent resplendence
Until...

POP!

Our bubbles redefined.

MERMAID MOMENT

There's a place I crave to be
Along a pathway, by the sea,
Where sugar sands sweep through the dunes,
Softly whispering their tunes.

To draw me on to water's edge,
Nestling in its rock pool ledge,
Calling me with dipped toes brave,
Mid-calf, then waist in rippled wave.

Serene, so calm, with floating hair,
Allowing thoughts to catch the air,
I wish that I could be there soon,
A mermaid in my own lagoon.

SANDY TOES AND ICE-CREAM CONES

This was a title of a chapter in my first book 'Finding My Way.' The sentiment of it came to mind in one of the many nostalgic moments I have had during the increased isolation of the last year. I do not think I am alone in this, judging by the type of programming popular on current television. I feel a yearning to be back at a time when worries were few and the freedom of childhood brought warmth to my days. Whether my own childhood or recalling moments when my children were young, thoughts of the seaside often soothe me. As the old song goes "I do like to be beside the seaside."

Sandy Toes & Ice-Cream Cones

'Dangle me Daddy,' our daughter said,
Hands aloft, waiting to swing over lapping waves,
Toes dipped in sandy embrace,
Sea breeze on the face,
'Wheee!' Jumping the waves.

A stroll along the water's edge in late afternoon,
Past rock pools and stripy deckchairs,
Remains of a castle wall falling,
Seagulls swooping and calling,
Anticipating a dive for a bag of chips.

The cool relief of a slap of sun cream applied,
A slow meandering flip flop walk,
The joy of a promised ice-cream,
A satisfying, swirling dream
Savoured, sat upon the harbour wall.

REFLECTION

This year we went for several walks,
My husband, dog and I,
Through crimson crunched leaves underfoot,
Sun hung low in the sky.

To be in autumn splendor,
Enfolded in its scene,
To pause beside a tranquil lake –
A stillness, peace, serene.

Where thoughts like leaves can float away,
Twirl and twist upon the air,
And muddy boots kick chestnuts,
Whilst the breeze kisses my hair.

These memories now are fading,
I don't want to let them go,
I wish we were still basking
Within that autumn glow.

FULL MOON

What draws the eye to stare upon the moon when its glow is full?
A beacon in the midnight sky,
A skipped heartbeat of mystery,
Watching us beneath, amongst our toil,
Returning our gaze with silent stare,
Softly hanging there...

SNOWFALL

Silence encapsulates

New covers old

Over the tarnished

Wrapped up in cold

Falling and floating

Awakening a smile

Linked to a childhood

Lain still for a while

VIEW FROM MY WINDOW

Each morning I raise the curtain on a new day,
My roller blind revealing the rooftop scene,
From my seat at the window,
The world sits outside,
Same scene, different season,
New day, new reason to watch for a moment...

From here, stretching out, are tower blocks and trees,
The hint of hills in the distance, before them
A church spire protrudes,
Piercing the sky,
And a child's cry shifts my gaze for a moment...

The foreground - a patchwork quilt of suburbia,
Haphazard gardens and higgledy sheds,
Some with no order,
Each marked with a border – I pause...

In this moment, my daily morning moment...

I have watched for a year, this view from my window,
Through snow and rain or radiant sun,
Silent at times, or full of sounds,
Colours and shapes shift,
Mood falls and then lifts, all in a moment...

ALTERED IMAGES

It takes tremendous effort to stand steady on shifting sands.

COUNTING BUTTONS

There have been many nights this past year when it has been hard to fall asleep. Once I switched from teacher to writer in 2018, I feel as though the writing switch in my brain has been stuck permanently on – phrases percolate within my mind, often disconnected from what I am doing. It is perhaps hardly surprising that instead of drifting off to sleep, the quiet of a dark bedroom beckons such phrases to dance about with more excitement. Some nights these phrases take quite a while to calm down and those are the nights when I usually get my best writing ideas.

This poem began on one of those nights. It contains many nostalgic references to my grandparents, for it started with a sudden vivid picture in my mind of their flat and our childhood visits to it.

Billy is a fiction, a flight of poetic fancy. But he represents all those who are struggling to make sense of this altered life we are all having to live now. He is the embodiment of my relief that my father is not still struggling with his dementia during this pandemic. He too lived in the flat the poem describes, on the top floor with his brothers – a family of five, in four small rooms and London stretching out beneath their feet.

Billy saw his grandparents

Every Thursday afternoon,

Running past the churchyard

Keen to arrive there soon.

He counted all the stone steps

On the climb to their top flat,

Always pausing half-way up,

To straighten his school hat.

He grabbed Nan's box of buttons,

Slung his satchel on the floor,

Paused to smell his Nan's meat pie

As he watched the teapot pour.

His Grandad chose a record

Of his favourite marching band,

And Billy held the buttons,

Turned them over in his hand.

34

Nan spoke about the weather

From her raindrop window seat,

Looking out across the rooftops

And the puddles on the street.

The box had many buttons,

With all sizes big and small,

Different colours, shapes and textures,

But Billy loved them all.

His Nan cleaned the tall houses

On the other side of town,

Worked long hours and kept the home too

Without complaint or frown.

His Grandad was a carpenter,

Told him all about the wood,

And Billy counted buttons,

And it made his world feel good.

35

For at school, he felt unhappy,

Counted bruises more than friends,

Didn't understand his lessons,

Felt relieved as each day ends.

"Billy Braithwaite" said his teacher,

Though Billy never knew why,

As Billy's mind was counting,

Counting birds fly in the sky.

***

Now Billy counts his buttons,

Though he only has a few,

He lines them up across his bed,

Does not have much else to do.

No-one comes to visit now,

Which he doesn't understand,

So Billy counts his buttons

And holds them in his hand.

36

BANANA BREAD REALITY

3 over-ripe bananas
A pinch of despair
Sugar
Flour
Dusty loaf tin from the back of the cupboard
Bananas bruising on the side
Butter – well there's spread
Are there eggs? How many?
Needed two...

No. They were scrambled yesterday.
Pretty soft bananas – 1, 2, 3.
Oven set
Don't fret, Laura makes hers every week
Tells me with her posts
Beautifully presented on a floral cake plate,
Laura's pictures, standing proud on Instagram

Slurp coffee and scratch head
How to make this everyone-can-do-it, delicious, wholesome
banana bread?
Got half a sliced loaf left 'til Friday
Grab two slices, slap spread on them
Mash bananas roughly in a bowl
That will do

Sprinkle...
Sod it
Throw some sugar in as well
Banana sandwich and more coffee
#Winning at this lockdown – can't you tell?

AND IN OTHER NEWS

This poem was written in February 2021, to reflect how the minutiae of day to day life in each of our social bubbles, has become our news. Without places to visit, events to attend, the luxury of being able to invite somebody into our homes – without all of these things, simple, little moments have become the news of our days. We are even telling others about it through our screens – we have become simultaneously both newscaster and viewer.

"Any news?" she said, centring her head
In their weekly Zoom screen call,
"Oh, not really dear, I'm just sitting here –
A bit fed up with it all."

With a nod and a smile, she sat back a while
To sip coffee from her cup,
Raindrops fell again on her windowpane,
"Oh dear, Mum," she said. "What's up?"

"Spoke to Blue-rinse-Lou, her from number two,
Had a parcel in the post,
She's been feeling low, but she thought, you know,
She would make herself a roast."

Sandra gave a sigh, she could almost cry –
Roast potatoes, Yorkshire pud,
All the family there, not an empty chair,
Back when Sundays still felt good.

"Do you remember Clive? Well, he's eighty-five
And he's just had his first jab,
Got a lift from Stan, in his delivery van,
Saved him calling out a cab."

The screen froze just then, playing up again,
With Mum's last words getting lost,
Has she fixed it yet? Bloody internet,
Oh, she's back, but looking cross.

"Have you seen the count? Such a large amount,
I can't watch the news no more.
Oh, Nadine dropped by with an apple pie,
Left it for me, by the door."

Sandra's take-away, left from yesterday,
Was an okay breakfast, right?
And it's safe to say, her 'Couch to 5K'
Is frankly out of sight.

"Saw Jane-with-the-twins, think she's looking thin
And she didn't say a lot,
I've not seen her Pete, up and down the street,
Not sure how much work he's got."

Sandra nods and sighs, as they sympathise,
Sees her Mum's on mute once more,
For a technophobe, she has learned a load,
All alone, behind closed doors.

"Sandra, how about you -had much work to do?
Are you fed up with this rain?
What do you think, dear, will it be this year?
Will they let us live again?"

"Hope so, Mum, guess so, it is hard to know"
Sandra wipes a tear-stained cheek,
Her cat gives a purr, ruffling his fur,
"Call you back again next week."

LOCKDOWN NURSERY RHYMES

This new spin on a few traditional nursery rhymes is my tribute to all those families combining working from home with supporting young children with their school work within a home context – trying each day to juggle and meet many needs.

Round and round the local park,
Dog leading the way,
One step, two step,
Walking every day.

***

Shall I put the kettle on?
Shall I put the kettle on?
Shall I put the kettle on?
It's time for tea.

Shall I put it on again?
Shall I put it on again?
Shall I put it on again?
And have another tea.

Sing a song of sixpence,
A new skill yet to try,
Four and twenty Zoom calls,
Trying not to cry,
When the day is over,
I'm heading for the gin,
You'll find me on the sofa,
So let the film begin.

***

One, two, three, four, five,
Tommy's class is streaming live,
Six, seven, eight, nine, ten,
Don't walk past the screen again,
What does he have to know?
Something the teacher said was so,
What if he gets it right?
There may be chips for tea tonight.

***

Twinkle, twinkle, where's the bar?
In the kitchen, not too far.
Up above the child lock high,
No more 'January – dry,'
Twinkle, twinkle, pass the wine,
I know it's only half past nine!

CODEWORD: FINE

A post from my blog 'Midlife Musings' written as thoughts about our mental health, something we will all need to put effort into supporting as time goes on. Currently it feels akin to a sleeping lion in the corner of the room, sooner or later it is going to wake up and I hope we are ready for it...

"How are you?"

"Fine, thanks. You?"

"Not bad, not bad..."

Does this sort of conversation sound familiar? It's the type of exchange that I have been part of many times over the years but now, more than ever, the absence of meaning within it has been pulled more sharply into focus. It's a convention of small talk to ask how a person is, usually without any expectation of receiving a complete answer. I have often wondered what the response would be to a full and honest answer. Then again, I am usually the one who is choosing to respond with a quick "fine" - it's the easy option, right?

'Fine' is the 'go to' response. 'Fine' means I don't have to think about other ways to respond. It spares others from having to listen to a list of my current worries and also spares me from having to admit that I am not actually 'fine' at all. I'm guessing that is mostly understood by all involved anyway. It's all part of the "keep calm and carry on" philosophy but where do we draw the line and recognise that we have to start paying attention to the elephant in the room? Surely there comes a time when we do actually have to talk about the issues in order to try to fix them.

This is true of any time but now there is the backdrop of this interminably relentless pandemic adding to that conflict. There are no end times and distinct cut off points in sight. Our goals are hesitantly set and then almost immediately, moved further away from us. So it feels impossible to set our own action plans as a way to manage any personal difficulties. How can we lay down markers for ourselves to achieve, when we are figuratively stuck in this bog, going nowhere, as the mass of self-doubt and anxiety pulls us down into the mud to hinder our way ahead?

Of course the word 'fine' does have its positive credentials. A quick look at a dictionary definition will tell how it indicates something of very high quality, like a fine wine that we would all be happy to toast with, or the report of fine weather forecast for a weekend ahead. Nothing ambiguous about those. I'm not sure that my type of fine day meets that criteria though. Here are my top ten moments of a 'fine day.'

1 manage to ignore the voice in my head telling me to stay under the duvet

2 squeeze myself into one of the few pairs of jeggings that still fit over my swelling tummy bulge and disguise what's left with a baggy jumper

3 accept that my hair will do, having scrapped the long wayward mess of it into a ponytail - it hasn't been cut for almost a year now and has more roots on show than any highlights that were ever added to it

4 feel good that I've got out of bed and am making my breakfast before 10 am

5 tell myself that my instant coffee in my favourite mug is just as good as the coffee shop experience that I used to revel in as I played out the role of writer in my head

6 face the daily dilemma in all of this - will I or won't I be able to drag words out of my head and onto a page to arrange into

something that may be of interest to someone?

7 look in the cupboard where biscuits and chocolates call to me, there are still quite a lot left over from Christmas to tempt me - one chocolate bar is okay, right?

8 after walking the dog around the legally-permissible local route, try to write again and manage to avoid the news and social media headlines of vaccines and death figures

9 cook dinner from the now overly familiar ingredients we stock each week, thinking as I stir fry the peppers or mash the spuds, of a time when we might go out for a meal and sit alongside people that we don't live with

10 stay up too late watching a stream of TV lifestyle moments, mildly amusing comedy shows, some celebrity walking a coastline or climbing a rock face, films from a different era, escapism to a different time or place, - anything that distracts the mind to help it to go off to sleep when I finally get off the sofa and into bed after midnight, to start off another fine day again the next morning and repeat it all again.

At this point I wish to make it clear that I am completely aware that this is indeed a privileged existence. I don't have to get on a crowded tube train, battle my way into work, or follow what must feel like endless restrictions or conditions within a workplace. I have food in my cupboards and a roof over my head and every day in this dystopian existence, I am grateful for this and saddened by stories of those who are struggling, missing out on furlough, and falling through the cracks and such. I heard this discussed a little in a recent podcast by Elis James and John Robins. The presenters discussed how some people are having to use their savings to weather the storm that we all find ourselves in. Agreeing that everyone is having a succession of rainy days but that "some people have been given umbrellas." How true, that we're not all experiencing this storm from the same viewpoint.

Still, I can only speak of my own experience, from my

viewpoint. So I have to ask if it is wrong to seek an end to this destruction or to be disturbed by the fact that I cannot do anything about it. As a mother, I want to be able to reassure my children that things will be resolved, to offer a brighter future. Mothers always make things right, don't they? I cannot do this though, I have no answers and no way to make everything okay. When asked what I think will happen and when I think we will start getting back to some sort of normal, I wish I could say what they want to hear me say. That everything will be fine. Can somebody please tell me this will be so and this time, can 'fine' mean just that - the best of something? Until then, a satisfactory day will have to do.

"How are you feeling?"

"Oh, I'm fine thank you. I'm still here and spring is coming and I'm absolutely fine."

IT'S GOOD TO TALK

'It's good to talk,' be it a cliché,
It's a driving human trait,
To connect that way,
To listen and say,
Find a way – communicate.

Talk of random things, often on a whim,
Of the big and of the small,
And to know by chance
That a random glance
Has the power to say it all.

Talk of fond memories, of a time we laughed,
Sometimes laughed until we cried,
Making sense or not,
As you lose the plot,
Sharing all that was inside.

Then there's times when there are just no words,
Not a single thing to say,
But to just be there,
Showing them you care,
And you made the time to stay.

Saying what you feel, sharing of that load,
To just get it off your chest,
May not solve or right,
But it casts some light,

Helps to go on with the rest.

'It's good to talk,' never mind cliché,
Don't be tempted to just wait,
Do it every day,
In some simple way,
Take that step – communicate.

HOPE

Hope can shine a light in the darkest of corners.

HAPPY BIRTHDAY

Here's to together times and smiling days,
Coffee cup chats wrapped in nostalgic haze,
Friends round a table sharing pizza and pud,
Laughing again and feeling good.

A day at the seaside, the breeze on our face,
Time to browse a shop at meandering pace,
To hugs and conversation, sat within the same room.
And actual celebrations without the need of Zoom.

A toast to love and friendship, habits to renew,
Singing round the candles – "happy birthday to you,"
Many little moments, together spread a smile,
May we share them all again someday, in just a little while?

WEATHERING THE STORM

We might all be in this same storm
But if we pause to think,
Some of us have waterproofs,
While others may well sink.

For some, the thunder's deafening
And circling overhead,
Others can watch the lightning strike,
Cupping cocoa from their bed.

For some, a distant rumble
Might interrupt a day,
But some are stuck in puddles
And they cannot splash and play.

If life's dealt you an umbrella,
Use it wisely and you'll find
Many others seek its shelter,
Look around you and be kind.

A HUG

There's power in a hug –
The connection of touch,
A collection as such of emotions.

Shared memories and thoughts –
Partner, family or friend,
Just to hold and to mend something broken.

Simplistic yet complex –
Though this may seem absurd
But this three-lettered word can speak volumes.

For only when missing –
Does its absence leave space,
Which you yearn to replace and keep giving.

This was written during the first lockdown, as part of my poetry collection: Diary of a Dizzy Peri. The sentiment behind it remains as strong as ever, hence its inclusion here too – hoping that we will soon be able to feel the benefit of a hug again.

WISH LIST

My Mum has been one of the many people, behind closed doors, shielding away from the unseen threat over the past year. Moving from complete isolation to being allowed a support bubble, but still mostly alone and inside her own space with her own thoughts, for almost a year now.

There have been days when the enormity of this has struck her, moments of sadness for what she continues to miss, but mostly she has kept going and kept cheerful. In that, I have found her inspirational. We are looking towards the hope that the next year brings, hopes of being part of a wider picture again. Although there are many hopes and wishes attached to what we would like to do when this is the case, when asked, all that my Mum says she would like to happen, is that she can be given a hug.

This next poem is therefore dedicated to Mum and the many others who have quietly continued to wait for a hug and for simple wishes to come true.

Shall we walk among the flower beds soon?
Watch the flight of bumble bees,
Spend an afternoon sat in a park,
With a picnic by the trees.

Shall we book a table at our favourite place?
With the family all together,
Tuck into a hearty roast,
Talk of little more than weather.

Shall we take a drive down to the coast?
Let the sea sounds cast their spell,
Stumble on the pebbles,
Have a tale to tell.

Shall we open our doors wide again?
And with them too, our arms,
Offer tea and hugs to visitors
And keep them safe from harm.

TIME

Me time,
We time,
Anything but us time,
Zoom time,
Clean a room time,
Hoover and dust time.

Walk time,
Talk time,
Kettle on and tea time,
Book time,
Cook time,
When will we be free time?

Ice-cream time,
Daydream time,
Soon to get a jab time,
Shout time,
Going out time,
Wouldn't that be fab time?

Keep on, cope time,
Dare we hope time?
Been a long, hard year time,
Hugging tight time,
Day and night time,
Thankful to be here time.

RUBY'S RIBBONS

This is a true story.

Well, most of it is. All stories are true for a while, for the time that you read them that is. For that is their special power and their magic. But real life has magic in it too, if you know where to look for it. Often it is found in the most ordinary of places, with ordinary people and ordinary objects. This then, is an ordinary, magical story and here is its truth.

It all began a few years ago, with a simple idea and, as we all know, the best ideas usually start from something simple. This one took shape when a lady called Clare took a few ribbons to Oadby Youth Centre. But perhaps it is better not to start at the very beginning, choosing instead to jump forward to a moment when the ribbons had been doing their work for a while. For that moment, we must picture a rainy Monday morning and a little café offering shelter and warmth.

***

Clare pulled a yellow ribbon from the collection in her bag. Clare — the lady with the vibrant red hair and personality to match, who sat each week in the corner of the café. From her favourite cosy spot, with coffee cup in hand, she could drink in both her warming frothy caffeine hit and her view of the tables dotted around the bustling café. This Monday morning she settled into her usual routine and watched the stream of people pausing their days to rest and chat. She smiled between her sips of coffee and her knitting, and all the while, her passion for her ribbon project grew.

Today, like most Mondays, it was not long before the ribbons on Clare's needles cast their spell. Slowly woven into an ever-growing scarf, sooner or later they captured the interest of an onlooker, drawing them nearer with each click of the size five needles.

"What are you doing?" asked Ruby, a little girl with ribbons of her own tied into two untidy bunches of her ash brown hair.

"Oh, hello," said Clare. "I'm listening to my ribbons." She held up the snaking scarf of ribbons in response to Ruby's question. Ruby tilted her head quizzically as she took hold of part of the scarf and began to run her thumb and forefinger along a silky ribbon that had caught her attention. Clare's infectious smile spread across her bespectacled face, encouraging Ruby to explore the ribbons further.

"I can't hear anything. Ribbons don't speak," stated Ruby with the unwavering confidence that eight year olds often possess.

"Well my ribbons do, they tell me their stories," said Clare. "They all have something to say."

"All of them?" Ruby's amber eyes opened wide. "What do they say to you?"

"Too many things to tell all at once, for I have so many of them," explained Clare, smoothing out the twisting, bumpy collection of ribbons currently hanging from her knitting needles. "Imagine if you had a whole shelf of books all shouting their stories out to you at once, that wouldn't be much fun would it?"

"It would be very noisy, worse than playtimes at school," said Ruby. "I don't like playtime, there's always too much noise."

"Well, that's the same with my ribbons, I suppose. They can't all tell their stories at once, so I only carry a few of them with me each day. All of these ones belong together in this section. It's called Freedom, do you like it?" asked Clare.

"Very much so," replied Ruby. "You mean this is the book of Freedom?"

Clare laughed and Ruby watched her eyes dancing. "I think that's a great way to describe my scarf – each part is like a book on the shelf, and all the ribbons are the words and chapters inside them. Shall I help you to hear the story?"

"Oooh yes please," said Ruby, as she moved her chair closer to Clare's and laid the scarf section across her lap. "I love stories, they can travel anywhere and when I hear them, they take me with them on their journeys."

"Well, let's see where this story takes us then."

With that, Clare began to tell Ruby all about the ribbons of the Freedom story. She explained that the yellow ribbon she was knitting today, was singing a song for a lady she had met. The song was called 'Tie a Yellow Ribbon' and brought back memories of a childhood holiday where the lady had built sandcastles and jumped over waves and sang the song loudly as she danced on the water's edge. Ruby could just imagine the scene and understood the feelings of freedom attached to it. She knew a little about the word 'Freedom' as she had heard it used at school in an assembly and she watched television programmes where presenters talked about animals running free. She had decided that she felt free whenever she found time to sit and quietly read, or when she watched the birds flying off from the bird feeder that swung on the branch of a tree in her garden. The more Clare talked, the more Ruby wanted to listen and to know about all the other stories that this kind lady's ribbons told.

"Will you be here tomorrow?" asked Ruby.

"Not tomorrow, but I'm here every Monday, adding to my scarf."

"Can I come listen to your stories again?"

"Of course. What's your name?"

"Ruby. What's yours?"

"Clare."

"Clare – the ribbon lady."

"Would you like to choose your own ribbon to add, Ruby? Then I can add your story to the scarf too"

"Am I allowed? I don't have much of a story to tell."

"Everyone has a story, Ruby. Have a look in my bag and see which ribbon will tell your story."

As Ruby examined the ribbons, their colours and textures, Clare explained how her scarf had grown over the months, with all the people she had met. She told Ruby how different people had chosen ribbons to add to the scarf whilst they shared their thoughts and feelings with Clare. Sometimes people had been very sad or lonely, and choosing a ribbon and talking about their worries had helped them to feel better. Sometimes there had been a happy event, a joyful song, or an exciting place that people wanted to remember and so they had rummaged in Clare's ribbon bag until they found the perfect one to speak for them. Ruby was captivated by the idea of all the ribbons and all the stories.

"How about this one, ribbon lady?"

"That's very pretty. Why that one?"

"Because it looks magical, just like you and your scarf."

"That's very kind of you."

"How long are you going to make your magic scarf?"

"I'm not sure. How long do you think I should make it?"

"Make it go all around the world. Everyone should hear your magic ribbons."

"That would be fantastic, wouldn't it? I'm not sure I can make that happen though."

"If you believe you can, then you will," declared Ruby, triumphantly.

"Well, I'd better add your ribbon and keep knitting then."

Ruby gave Clare the ribbon she had chosen, the pastel coloured, glittery ribbon that she had found as her treasure within Clare's ribbon bag. Then she jumped off her chair. Her mother was beckoning her back to their table and it would soon be time to go.

"Thank you, magic ribbon lady."

"You're welcome," said Clare as she began to weave Ruby's ribbon into the scarf. Ruby's story was one of many that she would add, one of many voices to be heard but one that would stay with Clare. She would never be able to knit enough to stretch the scarf around the whole world but perhaps Ruby was right. Stories can travel anywhere, if you just believe in them.

This is not the end of the story, for Clare is still knitting her Community Harmony Scarf. Still connecting with people, hearing their stories and finding just the right ribbons to carry their words to others. Ruby still loves her stories and looks for the ribbon lady whenever she returns to the café. Maybe one day they will meet again to hold the scarf together as they send its story around the world. Until then, we can all keep sharing our stories, for while one voice may be just a whisper, when we join our voices together, the resulting chorus cannot be ignored.

Illustration created by Zoe Honnor – a cosy armchair, magic knitting needles and ribbons weaving their stories around the world.

A PICTURE SPEAKS A THOUSAND WORDS

I spent some time scanning through a selection of photographs that I had posted on Instagram over the past year. Many tell a narrative of being confined to my locality – there are some from my garden, local parks or from mini celebrations held at home, necessitated by the restrictions that we have all had to follow. There are a few photographs though, of times when we were allowed to venture a little further for a day out here and there. Those were the shots that caused me to stop scrolling. Pausing at such images was like peering through a toyshop window as a child. Each one had significant memories and emotions attached to them and I wished I could somehow dive through my phone screen to be back in each of those moments. The saying often quoted is that "a picture speaks a thousand words." Some pictures definitely have that quality and power to them.

Often I post pictures and then poetry follows on from there. I feel a need to place my thoughts, responses and emotions alongside the photographs. They become a visual and poetic diary. Several of the poems contained within this book began with such a photograph and the experiences attached to the moment captured on the screen. I could add a selection of them here, but I guess they would not carry the same impact for you, as they do for me. I hope the poems speak for themselves and actually, may well evoke pictures of your own to attach to them. We are all holding on to our precious memories, our snapshots of shared times, the sort of times that we yearn to return to. Soon there will be more times to capture on our screens again - more smiles, more hope, more light.

An evening spent stargazing, sipping hot chocolate and sharing the smiles and hope of friendship.

ABOUT THE AUTHOR

Karen Honnor has had a life-long passion to write which has mostly focused upon her poetry and script writing in the past. With a few of her poems published and her scripts used by her local drama group, Karen always had a desire to write something more significant. Motherhood and a teaching career left little time for that but then beginning her blog and circumstances leading to her current career break would change all that.

With a long teaching career completed, Karen is now devoting time to her writing and to her family – husband, Stuart, grown-up children, Matthew and Zoe, and their furry cockapoo called Gizmo. Alongside all this, her usual commitments include much time with her drama group as Producer, Script-Writer and Choreographer. Though that has been put on hold for now, she remains in touch and promises to bring one of her bakes along when they next meet up in person.

Karen now has four books published, with her memoir and fiction writing supplementing her poetry. You can follow her writing adventure via her author website: karenhonnor.com.

Read on to find an excerpt from her recent novella, 'Unravelling'

1 JUST THE TICKET

Lucy brushed a tear from her cheek and allowed her gaze to focus through the blur onto the well-thumbed slice of the past that she was holding. Just a simple bus ticket. Insignificant at first glance and easy to discard as so many of its kind would have been in days gone by. Casually thrown away at the end of a mundane journey but this one was different, well it was to Doris.

A half-grin formed as Lucy recalled the day she had retrieved this. The vultures had already picked over the china and trinkets but you cannot put a price on all that is precious. Crouched in a corner of her Gran's dusty attic, Lucy had discovered the tin of random oddments, protected all these years by nostalgia and sentiment. It would have been so easy for this to have been scooped up with all the other scattered memories due to be cast aside during the house clearance. But Lucy sensed its significance.

Most people had stopped listening to Doris once she had been confined to the nursing home as her conversation lost its thread and her thoughts fox-trotted around. Not Lucy. She loved her Gran's stories and amongst their confused dance there was the sparkle of an odd gem of truth. At those moments the gentle pools of her gran's greying, blue eyes invited Lucy in. Just as a spool of old movie footage reveals a scene clicking frame by frame, she caught glimpses of the girl her gran used to be. Doris in her dancing days, in whirling petticoats with tumbling sandy brown locks catching the light as her feet marked the beat.

66

The rush of young love with a gaze exchanged across the dance floor may have become a faded memory for Doris but the tale of how they met, dodged the raindrops and held hands to take the bus ride home together, was her favourite to recall. In her rocking chair, crocheted blanket upon her knee and Lucy's wondrous 'treasure box find' placed beside a tray of tea, Doris was now content. The broken connections of life's confusion that usually frustrated Doris were strangely calm this afternoon. Lucy saw this peace reflected in the window pane's rivulets of rain.

With a determined effort Doris pressed the ticket into Lucy's palm, clasped her hand tight and returned her focus to the rain.

"Goodnight, sweetheart..."

Available in paperback and kindle versions on Amazon

©2020 ISBN: 9798570291096

Other titles available via Amazon –

ISBN: 978-1070372862

ISBN: 979-8643542551

Taken at Blenheim Palace, Oxford – 2020

(The day before our first lockdown.)